★ REFLECTIONS OF A ★
BLACK COWBOY

BOOK FOUR ★ MOUNTAIN MEN

★ REFLECTIONS OF A ★
BLACK COWBOY

BY ROBERT H. MILLER
ILLUSTRATED BY RICHARD LEONARD

SILVER BURDETT PRESS

Copyright © 1992 by Robert Miller
Illustrations © 1992 by Richard Leonard
All rights reserved including the right of reproduction in whole or in part in
any form.
Published by Silver Burdett Press, Inc., a division of Simon & Schuster, Inc.,
250 James Street, Morristown, NJ 07960.
Designed by Leslie Bauman
Manufactured in the United States of America
10   9   8   7   6   5   4   3

Library of Congress Cataloging-in-Publication Data

Miller, Robert H. (Robert Henry).
Reflections of a Black cowboy.
Includes bibliographical references (p. 80)
Contents: bk. 1. Cowboys—bk. 4. Mountain men
1. Afro-American cowboys—West (U.S.)—Biography—Juvenile literature.   2.
West (U.S.)—Biography—Juvenile literature.   3. West (U.S.)—Social life and
customs—Juvenile literature.   4. Cowboys.   5. Afro-Americans—Biography.
6. West (U.S.)—Biography.   I. Title.
F596.M646   1991
978′ .00496073022

[B]   91-8661
ISBN 0-382-24082-0 (lib. bdg.) ISBN 0-382-24087-1 (pbk.)

CONTENTS

PREFACE

Welcome to *Reflections of a Black Cowboy*. The books in this series were written to introduce you, the reader, to African-American people who helped settle the West. You'll meet cowboys, pioneers, soldiers, scouts, and mail drivers, and be part of history as our narrator the "Old Cowboy" remembers some stories from days gone by.

As young boys, my brother John and I would sit on the floor around my mother's favorite chair, waiting quietly for her to read us a story. She liked to read to us about faraway places and magical times. When I closed my eyes, I could see myself in the story—as a bystander or one of the main characters or often as the hero.

Like many black children growing up in the fifties, my heroes were drawn from the movies. Many of my favorite movies were westerns. Judging from what I saw in these movies, I figured there were no black cowboys. Most blacks had roles in the background as cooks or shoeshine boys or stable hands. Unfortunately, those weren't exactly the roles I had in mind for myself when I strapped on my play gun and holster outfit.

It was after one of those games of Cowboys and Indians that my mother told John and me a few new stories about her uncles, Ed and Joe Cloud. We thought "Cloud" was a strange-sounding name. Our mother explained that our great-uncles were cowboys who had traveled throughout Texas and Mexico. Often, they had to shoot their way out of trouble on cattle drives.

From that day on, John and I had a different perspective when we played our games of Cowboys and Indians. Instead of Hollywood movie stars, our uncles became our heroes.

This book is an effort to help define our cultural heritage and to pay tribute to Ed and Joe Cloud and all the other black men and women who helped tame the West.

Journey back with me now to that place called the wild, wild West, where you can be whoever *you* want. All you need is a fast horse, some boots, and a saddle. Now close your eyes—enjoy the ride!

Robert Miller

INTRODUCTION

In selecting the four men whose stories are included in *Reflections of a Black Cowboy: Mountain Men,* I've tried to paint a landscape that spans time and events during which African Americans made significant contributions to the development of early America.

I start with a man known simply as Esteban, because he came to America in 1528 as a Moroccan slave. The Spanish were the first and most active explorers of the New World, as they called the newly discovered continents of North and South America. To help them in their explorations, they took with them a number of Africans. Esteban, who is recognized as the first African to enter the land that is now known as New Mexico and Arizona, was part of a Spanish force that searched in vain for the legendary Seven Cities of Gold.

From Esteban our odyssey takes us to the discovery of Chicago, by a Haitian-born Frenchman named Jean Baptiste Pointe Du Sable. Jim Beckwourth is also included, because he was an African American who lived one of the most colorful lives that ever defined a "mountain man." He grew up when America was coming into its own and at a time when the tensions between the Indians and white foreigners were at an all-time high. Jim became chief of the Crow Indians and fought with them against a common enemy. His exploits warrant discussion, and my hope is that when you read about Jim you will want to know more about this intriguing African-American adventurer. In my view, "mountain men" are characterized by their unquenchable thirst for adventure. These African-American men relied on nothing more than their skills as hunters and their ability to understand the Indians. They never played by the rules of white society, which tried to impose on them a second-class status. Instead they were busy living their adventures and enjoying life. Fear of the unknown had no place in their lives; freedom and independence were what they sought.

George McJunkin, the last individual whose story is given in this book, was a somewhat "accidental" man. I must admit I had a difficult time placing him with the others. McJunkin taught himself to read and write. He also possessed a vast curiosity about archaeology and geology. His dream as a boy in the mid-1860s was to become a cowboy. For young black boys in Texas at that time, being a cowboy meant a life of hard work. Yet McJunkin's father never let him forget the power of knowledge and reading. Under his father's influence, George's interest in his surroundings was sparked, which eventually led him to discover the Folsom

Site in Folsom, New Mexico. The ancient bones George found there soon proved that Indians had been in North America for over ten thousand years, a discovery that laid to rest an old notion that the North American Indian had been in America for only three thousand years.

In studying this man's life, you come to realize that George McJunkin had to overcome "mountains" of obstacles like many African Americans today, but he never let circumstances stand in the way of his search for knowledge. That's why I chose to include him in this book. Now, find yourself a fast horse, saddle up, and get ready to ride with the mountain men.

SUNDOWN
REMEMBERS

One day, on his way up from Texas to Montana, the Old Cowboy came riding into the dusty town of Cimarron, New Mexico, followed by his loping old yellow hound dog, Sundown. It was a bright winter day with a hollow blue sky overhead and cold air whipping around them like an unwelcome visitor. As they reached the outskirts of town, they could see the Sangre de Cristo Mountains lying dark and mysterious in the background, far beyond the little ring of clapboard and adobe houses. The whole place seemed deserted, and the Old Cowboy slowed his pony to a walk as he surveyed the empty streets. When he came to the center of town, the Old Cowboy saw a cluster of folks huddled around the front door of a large adobe building.

"Come on, Sundown," he said to his canine trail partner. "Let's go on over and have a gander at this."

The Old Cowboy tied up his pony at the side of the building and went to a small door that was partly opened at the back. As he entered the hall he saw a beefy, red-faced man delivering a speech from a pint-sized stage at the front of the building.

"Men, we have got to do something about that spooky wolf, Two Toes. I've lost three of my best breeding bulls, I don't know how many sheep, and other livestock, too," said Ben Johnson, a wealthy cattleman.

"Me too!" said another cattleman. "I've tried everything, but that old timber wolf has outsmarted me every time!"

"He's one mean lobo," a third cattleman said, using the Spanish name for wolf. "I'm at my wits' end! I put out some poisoned meat, thinking he'd go for it. I'll be danged if he never touched the stuff, but he killed two of my best cows."

The crowd was getting riled up, and Ben Johnson raised his hand for everybody to sit down.

Just about that time a tall, lean black man walked through the door. "I'm looking for Ben Johnson," he said.

The crowd turned so quiet you could have heard a pin drop in a bale of hay.

The burly rancher came over to the black man and extended his hand. "I'm Ben Johnson," he said. Turning to the other ranchers in the audience he said, "This here's Mr. Willis Peoples. He's the man who's going to wax that no-good lobo Two Toes."

From the back of the room, the Old Cowboy examined the startled faces of the townspeople. It was clear they hadn't been expecting the hunter to be a black man.

Now the town treasurer, Johnny Barnett, stared hard at Ben Johnson, then at Willis Peoples, then back at Ben Johnson.

" 'Scuse me," he said to Willis, trying to sound polite. "I think what we all want to know is what makes you think you can catch this wolf when every other man has failed? And just exactly how much do you plan on asking for the wolf's hide if we decide to hire you on?"

With grim determination, Willis walked to the center of the room. "I'm charging nothing for this job," he said, and the townspeople gasped. "And the reason I'm gonna get Two Toes is that he killed my only son. I've been tracking the animal for a year now. I know how he thinks. I'm near bagging him, and he knows it. All I need is just a little more time to corner him and I'll take him down. All I want from you folks is a donation of grub to keep me going and one able volunteer to help me finish the job."

"Well," Ben Johnson said with a smile as he looked around at the other ranchers, "I guess we sure can accept your generous offer. Who would you like to help you?"

Willis walked up and down the aisle looking every man square in the eyes as he passed. He stopped short when he came to the Old Cowboy.

"I want you, mister," he said.

"I reckon I can lend you a hand," the Old Cowboy said. "Me and Sundown here are on our way back up to Montana, but we can take a detour for a month or so to help you do your biddin'."

The next day they were up at the crack of dawn to track Two Toes. They rode for five hours, zigzagging from river beds to mountain trails, all the time heading farther into the mountains. At a certain point, Willis realized that Two Toes had hooked up with a she wolf and doubled back in the direction of Oklahoma, so they turned tail and rode nonstop after Two Toes across the Great Staked Plains of eastern New Mexico, the Texas Panhandle, and into Oklahoma.

About three weeks later, around noon, they found Two Toes again among the reeds and sycamores of the Cimarron River in Oklahoma. Silently, Willis Peoples handed his field glasses to the Old Cowboy. The lobo was resting just across the river. When he saw the size of the animal, the Old Cowboy almost fell out of his saddle. The wolf was about as big as a buffalo and looked about twice as mean.

"We ain't gonna give him a rest," Willis said, as he drew his Winchester from his saddle holster. He steadied the rifle across a forearm and let rip two shots, which blew up fist-sized chunks of dirt a couple of feet from Two Toes. The sound of the shots echoed up and down the river valley like thunder falling from the sky, and the she wolf jumped into the air and ran off downstream. Two Toes ran after her for a few yards, then decided to let her go and turned tail to run upstream. Willis and the Old Cowboy spurred their horses and chased after him. Finally they cornered the crafty old lobo in a small cave located halfway up a cliff on the river's edge.

"He's plumb wore out," the Old Cowboy said, as he observed Two Toes through the binoculars. "He's lathered in sweat from tip to tail and his tongue is dragging the ground like a ball and chain."

"He's still plenty dangerous, mister," Willis said. "They ain't never meaner than when they're cornered."

When Sundown got a scent of the wolf he began to growl and he slunk through the bushes with his back set low to the ground.

"Now you stay back and cover me," Willis said to the Old Cowboy.

"Hey, boy," the Old Cowboy said when he realized what Sundown was doing. "Come on back here."

But it was too late. The old yellow mutt took off toward the wolf like a bullet from a Colt .45. Sundown galloped all the way to the mouth of the cave, where he was met head on by Two Toes. The two animals crashed into each other and rolled down the cliff, fighting tooth and nail. Dust was flying in so many directions it looked like a tornado had landed on the banks of the Cimarron River. Sundown ripped out Two Toes' right eye, and Two Toes grabbed the mutt and flipped him into the air. Sundown landed on a boulder with a whack and didn't get up. Dazed, Two Toes turned this way and that, his teeth reflecting the light of the sun, trying to get a bead on the man he heard crashing through the underbrush toward him. When he saw Willis, Two Toes jumped up in a mad burst of energy and charged him like a grizzly bear. Willis's rifle exploded three times—Crack! Crack! Crack!—and Two Toes crumpled into the deep bed of leaves near the river's edge.

The Old Cowboy rushed over to the boulder where his partner Sundown lay. The plucky dog had a bad gash on his neck, but he shook his head as he slowly came around. The Old Cowboy sewed up the wound, and in a day or two Sundown was up and on his feet.

Willis and the Old Cowboy tied Two Toes to one of their pack horses and dragged him all the way back to Cimarron. There Willis handled the townsfolk just like the professional mountain man that he was. Silently, he rode into Cimarron. When he had reached the center of town, he stopped and cut the rope that bound Two Toes to the pack animal. "This one's on me," Willis said. Then he turned, and with the Old Cowboy and Sundown at his side, rode out of town just as silently as he had come in.

ESTEBAN
AND THE SEVEN
CITIES OF GOLD

A*bout a month after they had left Cimarron with Willis Peoples, the Old Cowboy and Sundown arrived back home at their cabin in Montana. It was mid-December, and Mother Nature had laid a thick blanket of snow on the hills around the Old Cowboy's cabin. The Old Cowboy carried into the cabin a young fir he had cut down in the forest and lit a fire. Soon the place was cozy, and the Old Cowboy fired up his pipe and began decorating his Christmas tree.*

"You know, Sundown, running into Willis Peoples set me to thinking about other black mountain men who have roamed these hills. Our folks have been in these parts a long, long time. Let me tell you a yarn about the granddaddy of them all . . ."

His name was Esteban, which means Stephen in our language, and he was a black slave who was born in the north African nation of Morocco sometime around 1500. Now Morocco at that time was ruled by a sultan, and all of the folks who lived there were Muslims, that is to say, they were followers of the Muhammad, a religious leader who began the Muslim faith 'way back in the seventh century. Spain, which was just on the other side of the Mediterranean Sea from Morocco, was a Christian country and was at war with Morocco. In one of its raids into Morocco a Spanish force led by a man named Andres Dorantes captured Esteban. From then on, Esteban was Dorantes's slave.

Dorantes was a rich Spanish landowner, the kind of person who was not content just to sit back in Spain making money off his lands. So he jumped at a chance to travel to the New World to seek an even bigger fortune. See, the Spanish believed that this New World, discovered by the explorer Christopher Columbus in 1492, was a place of unimaginable wealth. Several tall stories had sprung up about places that the Spanish believed existed in North America. For one thing they believed that a ''fountain of youth,'' a spring that turned old people into young ones again, was located somewhere in the territory the Spanish had named Florida, the land of flowers. Farther west, the Spanish had heard tales from Indians of a City of Gold, a fabulous city in the desert whose buildings were made of gold.

On June 17, 1527, Dorantes set out on an expedition to the territory of Florida with two other men, Captain Alonso del Castillo, who was a friend of his, and Panifilo de Narvaez, the leader of the expedition. These three men sailed first to Cuba, where the Spanish had set up their main outpost in the New World. From there they set sail for Florida, where they hoped to find gold and figured they might even stumble onto the fountain of youth.

The expedition, a party of five hundred Spanish and African men, landed in Florida on April 7, 1528. On the deck next to Andres Dorantes stood Esteban, his Moroccan slave.

In those days, slaves served at the pleasure of their masters, but Dorantes had known from when he captured Esteban that there was something different about him. He carried himself like a man of royalty. He stood tall and straight as a Spanish lance, and when he walked he was as graceful as trees swaying in a summer breeze. Dorantes was proud to own Esteban; that's why he made him his personal servant. There was something else about him that also appealed to Dorantes—Esteban could be trusted. If the expedition discovered gold or other treasures, Dorantes would need someone he could count on to bring those treasures back to Spain.

Despite the men's high hopes, the expedition soon got bogged down in a mess of confusion. None of the big honchos—and few of the men—had much experience in planning a long expedition so far from home. As the days turned into weeks, and then months, food supplies dwindled and fights broke out.

"How long do we have to put up with this?" Dorantes asked his friend Castillo one day. "It's been more than two months since we landed, and I've seen no gold treasures— just snakes and mosquitoes."

"I know," Castillo said. "It's all the fault of Narvaez. He lied to us when he told us he knew Florida." Castillo patted the flank of his fine Arabian horse and pointed to Esteban and several other slaves who jogged alongside. "At least we have these to ride—unlike those wretches."

Several days later, as they passed through a low-lying plain covered in savannah grass, the Spanish ran into a hunting party of Timucua Indians. The Timucuas were tall and strong, altogether very impressive folks. When Narvaez saw these Indians, he shouted "Prepare for battle!" to his party. The Timucuas approached the Spanish warily. As they came closer, the Spanish noticed the glint of gold jewelry shining from chains and amulets the Indians wore around their necks and wrists. The flashing jewelry shone brighter and brighter as the Indians approached, until at last the reflections in the hot Florida sun all but blinded the Spanish.

The Spanish soldiers and gentlemen just stood there, gaping like hungry dogs in front of a T-bone steak at the gold the Indians wore. At last, one of the Indians broke the spell by walking over to Esteban and touching his skin. See, the Indians must have felt a kinship to Esteban, because his skin was similar to theirs. Not one to frighten easily, Esteban stood tall and stretched out his hand toward the Indian.

The Indian smiled and grabbed Esteban's hand forcefully. Esteban knew what the others really wanted to know, so he took charge of the situation. He touched the golden necklace of the Indian and smiled, signaling with his hands for the Indian to take it off. Those Indians were savvy characters and picked right up on what Esteban was doing. Slowly one of them took off a necklace and handed it to Esteban, who held it up, asking in Spanish, "Where did you get this?" As he asked, Esteban pointed in different directions. At first the Indians just followed whatever direction Esteban was pointing his hand. Then Esteban held the gold necklace in one hand and with his other hand pointed his finger at it, then pointed in two different directions. This time the Indians understood. At once, they all nodded their heads to each other in agreement, and turned and stretched out their arms inland, saying things in their native tongue to one another that sounded like the slap of cool water off smooth stones.

Esteban tried to give back the necklace, but the Indian pushed his hand away, a sign for Esteban to keep it as a token of friendship.

When the Indians had left, Andres Dorantes stretched his hand out regally toward Esteban, indicating that the slave should hand the gold over to his master. Esteban did as he was told, but he had stirred up some resentment among the Spanish gentlemen.

''I'd watch that slave of yours,'' Narvaez said to Dorantes a little while later. ''I think he may cause us trouble later.''

Dorantes, who was still angry with Narvaez because of his sloppy handling of the expedition, said nothing.

Spurred on by their greed for gold, Narvaez and the others rushed through the thickets and forests of the Florida peninsula. A new summer had begun. The air was thick and steamy, and the sun broiled off the men's backs. Food was still scarce, and the men were even hungrier than they had been earlier. In all, they were as upset and mean as a swarm of hornets, when one day a Spanish scout reported back to the main company about discovering a village of Apalachee Indians.

''I saw gold bracelets and silver rings,'' the scout told the others.

''We will attack immediately,'' Narvaez said.

The Spanish let out a whoop and rushed in a rabble toward the village. Some stopped to strap on their hot and heavy steel armor but others just picked up a sword or musket and high-tailed it down the path that led to the village.

The Apalachees, who had known the Spanish were there long before the Spanish had discovered their village, waited for the intruders in the forest near the village. As the Spanish rushed down the pathway, the Apalachees shot arrows at the raggedy groups of Spaniards, picking them off like shaking ripe apples from a tree.

In front of him, Esteban saw a Spanish soldier buckle and fall to his knees. As the soldier turned for help, Esteban saw an arrow sticking through the steel breastplate the man wore. Then two more arrows hissed from the darkness of the woods and ripped through the soldier's armor with sharp, metallic pings.

Farther along, Narvaez and the others ran back toward Esteban in terror. "Retreat! Retreat!" Narvaez screamed as he ducked and weaved between the bodies of his men. All that afternoon, the remnants of the Spanish expedition stumbled through the woods toward the beach, dodging parties of Apalachee warriors. By nightfall, only forty Spanish and African men were left alive. They were trapped at a mosquito-infested beach on a bay next to the Gulf of Mexico. The men, consumed by fear and with their torn clothes soaked in perspiration, huddled together under the cypress trees.

"Listen!" said Dorantes. "You hear anything?"

"I don't hear a thing," said Esteban.

"Me either," seconded Castillo.

"You think we outran them?" asked Narvaez weakly.

"In the morning, we must not hesitate. We have to build something seaworthy or we will perish," Castillo said.

The next morning the forty men were grateful to be alive. Taking what swords they had, Esteban and the others fashioned them into tools and cut down trees to build a crude ship. The men knew that their only hope for survival was to cast off in this vessel and drift westward across the Gulf of Mexico toward the Spanish town of Panuco on the Mexican side of the Gulf, more than one thousand miles away. To survive on the beach they were on, you had to be more stubborn than a Georgia mule. Each day, men died of disease and exposure to the rain and unrelenting sun. Still, the survivors kept building, until at last the boat was finished. As the men dragged the half-boat, half-raft vessel into the water, a hail of arrows from the Apalachees' bows rained down on them. The Spanish struggled out of the water to meet this surprise Indian attack, but the exhausted Spaniards had little hope of victory. Within an hour it was all over. Only four remained alive: Castillo, Andres Dorante, Esteban, and another Spaniard, who was named Cabeza de Vaca. They were captured by the Apalachees and enslaved.

It's strange how fate can twist around. After their capture, the Spaniards, who had been the masters, were now reduced to being slaves, and Esteban, who had been a slave for most of his life, was given more freedom by the Apalachees than he had ever had under Andres Dorantes.

The captives lived with the Apalachees for six years, learning their customs and their language. Esteban quickly became the favorite of the Indians. He was big and tall just like they were, and just as strong, but he had something else in common with those Indians that the other three men didn't: Esteban looked more like them. As he got to know their language better, they would ask him if he was a distant kin. He would laugh these comments off like they were jokes, and sometimes Esteban and the Indians ended up in playful tussles in which Esteban proved his fighting skills by taking on two or three of them at once. Each time, to the chiefs' delight, he won. As Esteban became more and more trusted by the Indians, he learned secrets from them about the surrounding territory, secrets he would soon share with the other captives.

One evening, when the Indians were holding a large powwow at their village, the four men decided to escape.

Esteban knew by now where the tribe kept their boats, and he guided the other four to the spot. As quiet as whispers in the dark, they pushed the boat into the water, jumped on board, and sailed westward out into the Gulf.

Unfortunately, neither Esteban nor the others had any idea of the distance between the territory of Florida and Mexico, a Spanish colony on the other side of the Gulf. For two years they drifted down the coast, dodging hostile Indians and begging food off of friendlier tribes. Often, if the tribe seemed open, Esteban passed himself off as a medicine man. By now he knew several Indian languages of those parts, and he knew how the Indians behaved with one another. For their part, the Indians were impressed with Esteban. They had never seen any creature quite like him: a tall black man wearing bright feathers and beads around his neck. To the Indians, Esteban was the leader of this scruffy hobo pack. The other three seemed nothing more than sidekicks.

One morning as they sailed down the coast in their little raft, the party was caught up in a violent storm. The sky got as dark as a hard-used frying pan, and before long their boat was dancing on the waves like a cowboy hanging onto an angry bull at a rodeo. In the afternoon the boat broke to pieces and the four men were cast into the sea.

"Castillo!" Dorantes cried as the breakers pounded him into the sand.

"I'm over here," Castillo replied, barely able to speak.

"Esteban!" Dorantes yelled again.

"Over here," Esteban responded, as he pulled himself from the surf.

"Where is de Vaca?" Castillo asked, after they had all pulled themselves onto the shore.

They didn't have to wait long for the answer. A minute or two later a group of Indians came out from behind a large sand dune with bows and arrows pointed at the beached men and with Cabeza de Vaca in tow. One of the Indians threw de Vaca to the ground and pointed a drawn arrow at his head. The other five ran up to the beached men and, letting out sharp war whoops, surrounded them with drawn bows.

"Who are they?" Dorantes asked Esteban.

"Attacapas," Esteban replied. "They are supposed to be some of the fiercest people on the Gulf Coast."

Slowly, Esteban rose to his feet. The five Attacapas surrounding the beached men jumped back and tightened the strings of their bows. Esteban could see the whites of their knuckles as they strained to pull back their bowstrings to full force.

Standing straight as an arrow, Esteban spoke to the Indians in a tongue they understood. "We have come from far away upriver. We have brought you medicine. We are medicine men, all of us," he said, smiling.

At that moment the Indians dropped their bows and arrows, and one of them came forward and spoke to Esteban. "You have brought medicine to my people, and we will help you, feed you. You are welcome here," said the Indian. As the Indians led them to their village, Dorantes asked Esteban what the Indians had said.

"We are to come to their village and heal the sick," Esteban said.

"We?" Dorantes asked.

"Yes, all four of us," replied Esteban.

Castillo looked at Dorantes and shrugged as they followed the Attacapas to their village.

Once they arrived at the village, the chief showed the four men some Indians who had come down with a sickness. "Use your medicine on these men. They have come down with evil spirits," he said to Esteban.

Esteban looked at Dorantes and the other two Spaniards. The men had begun to sweat and stared back at him with blank, nervous faces.

"Now what?" Cabeza de Vaca asked Esteban.

"I'm not sure," Esteban said.

The Indians watched the four men closely as they spoke to one another.

"What did you do in Morocco when someone was sick?" Dorantes whispered out of the corner of his mouth.

"A doctor came and applied herbs."

"But we have no herbs," de Vaca said.

Castillo was becoming very nervous and upset. "For heaven's sake," he said, "think of something."

At that moment Esteban snapped his fingers, then, with a flourish, made the sign of the cross in the air. Kneeling in front of the sick person, he chanted the Lord's Prayer in Latin.

"Esteban, have you gone mad?" Dorantes asked. Castillo's knees buckled and he looked as if he were about to faint.

"Follow me," Esteban said. "Do just as I do and we'll get out of this alive."

Cabeza de Vaca, who was convinced that God had chosen him for all these hardships for a reason, immediately began to recite the Lord's Prayer in unison with Esteban. Soon, so did Dorantes and Castillo. Slowly, one by one, following Esteban's lead, the three Spaniards dispersed among the crowd, chanting and waving their arms in the air and blowing into the faces of the sick. Convinced of the power of these strangers, first one, then another and another Indian rose and proclaimed himself cured. Esteban looked at the others and winked. "Perhaps your God has much power after all," he said. From that moment on, the Attacapas honored the four men, but they reserved their highest honor for the man they believed was the chief medicine man, Esteban.

Esteban learned from the Attacapas that he and the others had landed on an island off the mainland. The Spanish nicknamed this place La Isla de Mal Hado, the Isle of Bad Luck. Later it became known as Galveston Island, on which the city of Galveston, Texas, is located today.

After the party spent a few weeks with the Attacapas, it was time to move on. Esteban explained to the chief that they needed a boat so that they could continue down the Gulf of Mexico and reach the Spanish settlement of Panuco.

"If you go that way, you will run into the Karankawas. They are on the warpath now. I know another way, through the mountains; my warriors will show you," said the chief.

One of the chief's scouts showed Esteban and the others a path that led westward through mountains never seen before by a Spanish or African man.

"Look at the view," said Dorantes. "I never saw such a beautiful sight. Not even in all of Spain has the land looked so green." Marching on through the mountains of what is now western Texas and northern Mexico, they passed from the lands of one Indian tribe to another, curing the sick. Word spread ahead of them about a group of medicine men led by a big, tall African, and they were offered warm welcomes and treated well everywhere they went.

They stayed for a while in northern Mexico, probably near the present-day city of Juarez, before turning north to trek across the mountains and deserts of New Mexico and Arizona. Somewhere in that area an old Indian chief pulled Esteban aside to chew the fat. "There is a trail over there," the old chief said, pointing northward, "that leads through the mountains to seven large villages filled with gold." Esteban had heard other stories from different Indian groups about this place, which many called the Seven Cities of Cibola. He burned into his memory the direction the Indian chief had pointed out, and vowed to himself that he would return and find these cities. Before they left that village the chief gave Esteban a large hard-shelled gourd, called a calabash rattle, used for ceremonial purposes. "Take this, it will bring you good fortune," said the old Indian. Waving farewell to the Indians, the four men once again set out into the vast desert.

This time the group turned south and walked through the rugged Sierra Madre mountains in the area that is now northwestern Mexico. One day, as they crested the peak of the mountains, they caught sight of the ocean.

Cabeza de Vaca fell to his knees. "Praise God!" he said. "Our struggle is almost over."

The body of water the men saw turned out to be a gulf off the Pacific Ocean, which is now called the Gulf of California. The men marched to the beach as fast as they could and threw themselves into the surf. They had no idea where they were, but somehow they convinced themselves that a Spanish settlement was near.

About a month later, in March 1536, Esteban spotted Spanish soldiers along the banks of the Sinaloa River in western Mexico.

"Over there!" he shouted. When one of the explorers turned in Esteban's direction, he quickly drew his sword. You can understand why. Here was an African man standing over six feet tall, waving a huge calabash rattler and wearing brightly colored feathers around his head and waist, with a deerskin just covering him to his upper leg. Dorantes and Castillo were close behind. The Spanish explorers approached these strange-looking men as carefully as a cat edging up to a rattlesnake.

"Who are you?" asked one soldier.

"Spaniards!" yelled Castillo.

The soldiers looked at each other in disbelief.

"We are all that is left of the party of Panifilo Narvaez," Dorantes added.

Now the soldiers were truly astonished. "That group was completely wiped out eight years ago," one of them said.

"Yes," said an excited Cabeza de Vaca. "Wiped out, all of them. Except for us. We are alive. By the grace of God we have survived."

The soldiers took them back to the mission town of Culiacan. There they rested, and, except for Esteban, all changed into European clothes and were sent to Mexico City to report to the Spanish viceroy, Don Antonio de Mendoza. In the chambers of the viceroy, Dorantes, Castillo, Cabeza de Vaca, and Esteban told the story of their journey into unknown territory. While listening, Mendoza couldn't take his eyes off Esteban's clothes, especially his gold bracelets.

"Gentlemen," the viceroy said, "I am fascinated by all of this, and of course, I'm saddened by what happened to Narvaez." Mendoza walked around his chambers dressed in a burgundy velvet jacket, black silk pants, and black knee-high riding boots, smoking a long, thin pipe. "But I must admit, I'm even more intrigued by your story, Esteban, about the Seven Cities of Cibola. I have heard rumors of such a place by some of the Indian slaves, but I dismissed them as rubbish. Can you swear to this, that such a place exists?"

"I can only swear, my lord, to what the Indians told me and showed me," said Esteban.

"Can you find this place again?" asked an anxious Mendoza.

"Yes, my lord!" said Esteban.

Mendoza walked around the room with his hands folded

behind his back, then stopped. "Gentlemen, how would you all like to go back and find this place? You will be handsomely rewarded and will be honored for your service to the Spanish crown," said Mendoza.

Standing in front of the viceroy, Dorantes, Castillo, de Vaca, and Esteban spoke among themselves, then turned to the viceroy. "My lord, it is the decision of us all, except Esteban, to return to Spain. We are not convinced about this city of gold, and we long for our homeland," said Castillo.

The viceroy said nothing for a moment, "I believe there is such a place," he said finally, "but if you don't want to be a part of this, that's your decision. But what about Esteban? Dorantes, he is still your slave. Do you speak for him?"

"Esteban has been with me for over eight years. He is trustworthy. If you wish his services, I will sell him to you," Dorantes said. "Then it is done!" the viceroy said. "Prepare your things. A ship leaves for Spain at dawn tomorrow. In the meantime, Esteban and I will talk some more about these Seven Cities."

An expedition to find the Seven Cities of Cibola was quickly organized. On March 7, 1539, Esteban and friar Marcos de Niza, who had been appointed by Mendoza to oversee the expedition, headed out into the mountain from Culiacan. Even though Esteban had only changed one master for another, he figured his chances at freedom would be much better in this New World than back in Old Spain. He also knew that the success of this new expedition relied totally on his memory and his ability to get along with the Indians. Dressed in his bright red and yellow feathers, with bells on his legs and arms, and carrying his calabash rattle, which signified his reputation as a medicine man, Esteban led his band of explorers like a king looking for his throne.

Retracing his path, Esteban led his party to the Indian

village of Vacapa, near the present-day town of Fairbanks, Arizona. There the friar, Marcos de Niza, called the party to a halt. "We will rest here until Easter," said de Niza.

Esteban didn't agree. The friar was as slow as molasses on a cold day, and Esteban wanted to find the Seven Cities as soon as possible. "We must go on," Esteban said, that night around the campfire. "The rains will come soon, and we can't lose any more time."

"Do what you must, my child," the friar said, "but I'm not going any farther. This was Mendoza's idea, not mine. Let me know when you've reached this City of Gold so that I can report back to him."

"How do you wish me to tell you when I've found Cibola?" Esteban asked.

The good friar rubbed his fat chin a moment. "Ah, yes. You will send one of your Indian guides back carrying a wooden cross. The closer you get to this city of Cibola, the bigger the cross. When you've found this city I don't want you to enter until I reach you. Understood?" asked de Niza.

Esteban understood, all right, but he had plans of his own. When he struck out the next morning with a few Indian scouts, he was finally on his own for the first time, and it filled him with great pride. He had come to the New World as a servant of Dorantes, and after eight years in the wilderness, during which he had saved the lives of his master and others, had been rewarded by being sold to a new master. In the wilderness he was his own master, and he made up his mind he'd never be a slave again.

From village to village the sound of reed flutes, shell fifes, and fish-skin drums followed this tall, bearded African who carried a large calabash rattler. Like rolling tumbleweed caught up in a dust devil, his disciples grew as the Opata Indians and others joined him. Beautiful Indian maidens and warriors all jumped to follow Esteban's enchanted trail for Cibola.

First one chieftain then another pointed him along the path to Cibola. At each stop he carved a cross, each larger than the last, to be carried back to Friar de Niza. Night after night his group built bonfires and chanted and danced under the desert stars until they fell asleep exhausted. And each morning they awoke with an almost magical renewal of energy, which they saw as a blessing from their medicine man, the greatest spiritual leader of them all, Esteban.

As the group neared Cibola, Esteban and his band began to be watched by silent scouts stationed along the rims of the canyons and high in the mountains. Esteban's party had by now traveled into the mountains of what is now eastern Arizona, and they would soon pass into the western part of what is today the state of New Mexico. The observers watching them from above had been sent by the chieftain of the Zuni tribe, whose ancient cities located on the tops of seven mesas (high flat-topped mountains) were together known as Cibola. The Zunis didn't take kindly to having outsiders intrude on their territory, and they especially didn't like this imposing African and his mob of excited followers. In their majestic cities the Zunis discussed what to do about Esteban and his outfit.

Meanwhile, back at his base camp, Friar de Niza was getting about as worked up as a jackrabbit on loco weed by the bigger and bigger crosses that Esteban's Indian porters kept laying at his feet. When at last an Indian stumbled into Vacapa carrying a cross as big as Esteban himself, de Niza could contain himself no longer. "Where is Esteban?" he demanded harshly of the messenger.

"Thirty days from Cibola," the Indian said. "They say the storehouses there are filled with gold and turquoise."

"Get a scouting party ready to move out in the morning," shouted de Niza. "We don't have time to waste. I must be there when Esteban enters the Cities of Gold."

As de Niza prepared to rush off after Esteban, he and his group had come in sight of Hawikuh, the first of the Zuni Cities of Gold. To show that he came as a friend, Esteban relied on the habits he had learned when entering new Indian villages. "I must give them something special, so they think I am special," he thought.

"Take this into the village," he said, handing a messenger his ceremonial calabash rattle, which had been given to him as a gift many years before by the Attacapa Indians. "Give it to the big chief." Then Esteban sat and waited for the joyous welcome that always came when he entered a strange village for the first time.

The hours passed as slowly as a midsummer's day in Kansas, but the messenger didn't return. At last he appeared on the horizon, his hands empty and his feet dragging in the dust.

"Where is the calabash?" Esteban demanded.

"Their chief threw it to the ground and crushed it with his feet," the messenger said. "He says whoever brings this brings death to himself, and all who stay."

At the time, Esteban had no way of knowing that the Indians who had given him the ceremonial calabash were long-time enemies of the Zunis. Looking over his followers, who stared back at him with forlorn eyes, Esteban's heart began to sink like a stone in a deep well. Mendoza and de Niza were all counting on him to bring back news that the Seven Cities of Gold were real and not just another pipe dream. But something else worse than this ate at Esteban. In all his years of traveling throughout the country, he had never been refused entrance to any Indian village, and this gnawed at his pride. The Opatas had warned Esteban to be careful with the Zunis, that they could be a dangerous people. "I will go in myself," Esteban told his followers. "They will listen to me." Then turning to an Indian runner, he said, "Go, send word to de Niza. Tell him I have found the Seven Cities of Gold, and that he must hurry if he wishes to enter with me."

With all the courage of an African lion, Esteban walked into the village of the Zuni Indians. He had been in close scrapes with death many times, and every time had lived to talk about it. He was sure this would be no different.

As he walked away from the campsite, his followers could hear the sound of the bells on his feet ring more and more softly until finally they were heard no more.

Curious to see what was going to happen, one of the braves ran silently behind Esteban and hid among the boulders at the edge of the Hawikuh mesa.

It was late afternoon as Esteban walked into the settlement, and the brick and mud buildings had turned golden in the fading light. This was the gold the Indians had spoken of, the only gold the Zunis possessed—the lush color of the town at the end of the day.

Zuni warriors came out of their houses and formed a gauntlet, through which Esteban was forced to walk. As he was halfway down the line, the chief, who stood at the end of the gauntlet, shouted an angry command. The braves suddenly began to strike Esteban with their axes and knives. The first few blows sliced him up something awful, but he broke free and ran back the way he had come. But the Zuni warriors were swift and caught him at the mesa's edge. They speared him several more times, stopping only at the orders of their chief. Slowly the chief walked over to where Esteban was struggling to hold himself upright. The chief said something to Esteban that the brave hidden among the rocks couldn't hear. Esteban seemed to wave his hands in the air as if making the sign of the cross, then he blew into the air and chanted. The chief stepped back and barked an order, and the braves came down on Esteban like hawks on a rabbit. In a few minutes it was all over, and the African sorcerer lay dead.

When Friar de Niza heard this story several days later, he stopped in his tracks and high-tailed it back to Mexico City. When he returned he repeated the old stories about the Seven Cities filled with gold, cities that in fact he never saw.

The Old Cowboy straightened up when he had finished telling this story and tossed another log onto the fire.

"Time to hit the hay," he said to Sundown. "We've had a pretty full day, I'd say. Besides, the day after tomorrow is Christmas, and we got some work to do before then."

JEAN BAPTISTE POINTE DU SABLE: FOUNDER OF CHICAGO

Sundown and the Old Cowboy *woke up at first light the next morning. As soon as he had rekindled the fire inside his cabin, the Old Cowboy went to work preparing a selection of meats in his smokehouse for a Christmas feast he was going to host for his old Sioux friend Chief Two Hawks. He had known Two Hawks now for twenty years, and they had spent many a month together in the wild, hunting, fishing, and trapping. When he had finished setting the meats to smoke, the Old Cowboy ambled back to his cabin. The sun had come out, and as he sat in his rocker by the window, gazing at the snow-covered mountains and thinking about the story of Esteban, he remembered a tale of another black man who had come to live in the wilds of America many years ago—not so long, in fact, after Esteban had died.*

"Sundown, a long time ago this land was pretty much wide open forest and prairie, from sea to sea. Why, by the 1700s white folks had only managed to throw up a few cities on the whole North American continent, and most of these were right on the edge of the land, near the sea, where they could be easily resupplied by ship from Europe. Several European countries had carved up North America between themselves. The English took most of the East Coast, the Spanish laid claim to Mexico and a good chunk of the West, and in between these two the French had grabbed a handful for themselves. Their spread extended from what is now Louisiana all the way up the Mississippi River to Canada and as far west as the state of Washington now. This parcel, which the French named New France, had its hub as the city of New Orleans, at the mouth of the Mississippi River on the Gulf of Mexico.

French soldiers, planters, explorers, and freebooters and pirates of all nationalities poured into New France, hoping to strike it rich by farming and trading. Bit by bit, they made their way up the Mississippi deep into New France. Of all these characters, the most colorful and ambitious were probably the trappers. There was one fella who was especially good at trapping and built himself a powerful fur business on Lake Michigan. Fact of the matter is, Sundown, this adventurer built the first house at a spot the Indians called Eschikagou, along the banks of Lake Michigan. That was way back in 1774. My, that place sure has grown since then. These days people call it Chicago.

This fellow was a black man by the name of Jean Baptiste Pointe Du Sable. The way I heard it, Du Sable was born in St. Marc, Haiti, around 1745. His father, Pointe Du Sable, was a young and adventurous French sailor, and his mother, Suzanne, was a freed slave from the Congo.

In those days, one of the quickest ways for an ambitious young man to make his fortune was to join up with a pirate crew, which is what Pointe Du Sable did soon after Jean Baptiste was born. The vessel he shipped out with was commanded by an African captain named El Negre, whose boat was called the *Black Sea Gull*.

Because he was away at sea for long periods of time, Pointe Du Sable didn't have much opportunity to see his son grow into manhood. During one of Pointe Du Sable's cruises, marauding Spanish pirates descended on St. Marc. Most of the men were out at sea on the *Black Sea Gull*, so the Spanish buccaneers easily stormed the town, as the women and children ran away screaming in terror.

As it happened, this Spanish raid occurred just as the *Black Sea Gull* was due back home. Jean Baptiste had been on the cliffs outside of town watching for his father's ship when he saw the Spanish advancing on the town from the opposite direction. Running blindly toward the town, Jean Baptiste was met by fleeing townspeople.

"Run, run!" they shouted. "The Spanish are killing everyone in the village."

Ignoring the danger, Jean Baptiste raced back to St. Marc, dodging Spanish pirates in the streets. At last he came to his own house. Bursting inside, he found his mother lying dead on the floor, the victim of a cutlass blow across her neck. In confusion and despair, Jean Baptiste tried to think of what he should do as the Spanish raged through the town outside. "I must go back to the cliffs," he said to himself at last, "and warn the *Black Sea Gull*."

By the time he had reached the cliffs again, Jean Baptiste could see the sails of the *Black Sea Gull* on the horizon. A full breeze was blowing that day, and the ship quickly moved toward the shore.

Jean Baptiste stripped off his shirt, gulped a deep breath, and leaped from the high cliff into the ocean. "I must warn them, I must warn them'' were the words that young Du Sable kept repeating in his head with every stroke of his arms.

Aboard the *Black Sea Gull* the crew stood relaxed and glad to be home. At sea three months, they had plenty of loot and rum to celebrate once their ship pulled into harbor. From his command post on the captain's deck, El Negre cautiously scanned the inland areas and coves. Suddenly, far away he saw a dot splashing in the swells, and like thunder rolling from the sky, he shouted, ''Man overboard! Man overboard!''

His crew moved quickly with practiced ease. A rope shot out from the bow, landing in the water a few feet from young Jean Baptiste's grasp. As the boy struggled to grasp it, El Negre noticed the tail fin of a man-eating shark cutting through the water. That old shark was bearing down on Jean Baptiste as the men on the ship pulled him in with all their might. ''Hang on, young fella!'' shouted the ship's crew. Up on the captain's deck, above his men, El Negre swiveled a harpoon gun, aimed, and like a flash of light that stick whistled through the air, slicing through the shark's left side.

Turning over and over in the water like a tumbleweed in a Texas tornado, the shark was hit a second time. Leaping into the air, the shark shimmied in a dance with death, then plunged into the ocean, where it disappeared into a watery grave. Coughing and spitting ocean water out of his mouth, young Jean Baptiste was pulled on board the *Black Sea Gull*.

''What do we have here?'' asked one old crew member.

''By George, it's a little fella,'' laughed another, poking a finger in Jean's belly.

As they all crowded around, a familiar voice cut through the crowd like a timber wolf howling in a canyon. ''Jean? Jean, is that you?'' asked his father. ''Spaniards. Papa.

They're burning St. Marc. Their ships are hiding in the coves, waiting for you!'' shouted young Du Sable.

Hearing this, El Negre climbed down from the captain's deck, his eyes boring into young Du Sable. Before he could say a word, Pointe Du Sable spoke up. ''This is my son, Jean Baptiste Pointe Du Sable. He brings word that the Spanish are hiding in the coves to attack us, and that they have already attacked St. Marc,'' said Pointe.

El Negre wasn't a man to waste time on decisions. ''We must leave here immediately,'' he said. Turning to his crew, he shouted an order: ''Sail ho!'' and the crew hurried into action.

Pulling his son aside, Pointe Du Sable asked cautiously, ''Your mother, is she . . .''

''Yes, Papa, they killed Mama,'' answered young Jean Baptiste. His father was a strong man who had cheated death more than once, but when he heard that his beloved Suzanne was dead, he turned his head away and wept.

Jean Baptiste Pointe Du Sable would never live in Haiti again. To escape the Spanish, the *Black Sea Gull* sailed to France, where Pointe Du Sable enrolled his son at St. Cloud, a boarding school outside Paris. By 1764, at the age of nineteen, Jean Baptiste had graduated from St. Cloud and faced the decision about what to do with his life. Around this time his father died, so the young man found himself alone in the world, with a number of possibilities open to him.

At this time many stories were going around in France about the French colony in North America known as New France. One evening, after hours of gabbing, Jean Baptiste and a school friend, Jacques Clemorgan, decided to head out for New France to seek their fortune. Pointe Du Sable had left Jean Baptiste a small schooner called the *Suzanne*, and the two friends resolved to sail to the New World in it.

Most of the voyage was surprisingly easy. Young Du Sable was as at home on the sea as a bronco buster is on a strange horse. On April 12, 1764, he and Jacques spotted the coast of what probably was New France.

"Are we lost, my Captain?" asked Jacques.

"If we are, it's not by much," Du Sable said as he peered through the hazy air toward the far sliver of rich green that marked the shoreline. "We're looking for the mouth of the Mississippi River," he added.

"And how do we know when we have found it?" Jacques asked.

"By the mud," Du Sable replied. "They say the color of the water at the river's mouth is muddy for as much as sixty miles out to sea."

As the afternoon wore on, the sky began to change. The winds, once calm and mild, were getting as restless as a corralful of anxious mustangs. The flapping of the sails made a sound like a flock of pelicans flying overhead, and the *Suzanne* began to bob in the rising surf. Lightning flashed across the sky as sheets of rain whipped across the ship's bow.

As the wind picked up, Du Sable grabbed the wheel of the *Suzanne* like a cowpuncher grabbing his favorite mount.

"What do you want me to do!" Jacques shouted.

"Get below!" Du Sable screamed over the howling winds.

"I'm staying here!" Jacques screamed back, but Du Sable couldn't hear him and could barely see. The *Suzanne* dipped into the ocean and was hurled into the air, nearly capsizing, as she mounted the crest of the wave. Du Sable, water slapping him in the face, held on to the wheel with all his might. In the distance, at the very edge of his vision, he saw

something coming at him that gave him religion in a hurry. It was a tower of water bigger than any building in Paris, and it sounded like a freight train moving at a hundred miles an hour.

"Hang on!" he screamed to Jacques, who clutched the railings open-mouthed as the tower of water hit the *Suzanne* and split her in half.

After the wave hit them, both Du Sable and Jacques Clemorgan managed to grab hold of a piece of the ship's mast. Several hours later they were washed ashore.

All night they lay on the beach, exhausted. The next morning, when Jacques tried to stand he fell down like a sack of potatoes. Du Sable, who was already up and about, saw his friend fall.

"Jean, it's broken. I cannot walk!" shouted Jacques. Du Sable hurried back to his friend and looked at his leg. "Climb on my back," he said. "I will carry you." Jacques didn't want to do this to his friend, but he had no choice. They got to the top of a hill and found there grassy slopes and moss-covered trees. Pushing the moss away with his hands, Du Sable saw a wide river.

"This is it," he said excitedly. "This must be the Mississippi." They waited down by the river's edge for three days, but nothing sailed past except deadwood. Jacques's leg had swollen up to the size of an Arkansas watermelon in July, and he was sweating something terrible. "Surely a boat must come today, Jean," whispered Jacques. "I hope so, my friend," Jean replied. The sun was high and bounced its reflection off the water like a mirror. Du Sable was becoming very worried about Jacques's leg.

Just then, out of nowhere, a vision came streaming around the bend. Jean blinked and looked again. It was a ship. He jumped like a jackrabbit running from a hungry wolf, waved his hands, and shouted in French. Then, not waiting for them to respond, he jumped in the water and started to swim for the ship.

Even though the river's current was strong, Du Sable was a powerful swimmer, and he managed to make it to the ship. As he pulled himself on board, he was met by a startled crew member.

"Who are you?" the crewman demanded.

"I am Jean Baptiste Pointe Du Sable. I am a Frenchman," he said proudly. Then he explained that he had a wounded friend stranded on the shore.

The captain of the vessel, a Mr. Jensen, came over to see what the disturbance was. When the crewman explained what Du Sable had told him, the captain at first was suspicious. Jensen's ship, the *Helsinger*, a Danish vessel, was now at a lonely stretch of the Mississippi. This young black man, even though he spoke well, might be a runaway slave or even worse, a pirate. However, something about the way Du Sable carried himself convinced the captain to send a boat ashore for Jacques.

Once Jacques was on the ship the captain felt more confident that he had made the right decision, especially after he saw that Jacques was a white man. Medicine was applied to Jacques's leg and he slept like a newborn calf.

The next morning, Du Sable was full of energy. New Orleans was just around the bend, so he climbed up the main mast to take a look. As the ship came around another river bend, Du Sable saw many small boats loaded down with trading goods, and canoes, flatboats, fishing shacks, and shops all lined up along the wharf. Farther along, the city of New Orleans was surrounded by a wooden wall. A small gap in the barricade allowed him a glimpse inside to a tropical vista of palm trees and a few white buildings. When his feet hit the ground, he heard cannon fire. Quickly he dove for cover. Some of the crew began to laugh, and one of them explained, ''That was Fort St. Charles. They always do that when a ship is docking—now everybody knows we're here.''

Jacques and Du Sable found a room in a boardinghouse run by a Mrs. Lafontaine, a once wealthy widow who now was down on her luck. From her, Du Sable discovered that they had landed in New Orleans at a dangerous time. Rumors were sweeping the town that the French king had sold New France to the Spanish. Furthermore, Mrs. Lafontaine warned Du Sable that because he was black he might be shanghaied on the streets and sold into slavery, even though he was a free citizen of France! Many free blacks had suffered this fate. Some were mistaken for runaway slaves, and others were only accused of being runaway slaves, by unscrupulous slave traders who wanted nothing more than to turn a profit from human misery.

Carefully, Du Sable looked for work around town, and he quickly discovered that the pay for black men was half what it was for whites. One day he heard that a trading company was hiring trappers and traders to send up the Mississippi to the northwestern outpost of New France, which was a hamlet called St. Louis.

When Du Sable got over to the hiring place, he found a line so long it could have wrapped around the state of Texas. By the time he got to the man in charge, the sun was almost setting.

''Can I help you?'' the foreman said, without even looking up.

Mustering his courage, Du Sable said, ''I am a seaman, and I have experience with Indians. I can be very valuable to your company.''

"Sorry, we don't have any more openings. Next!" the boss shouted.

Du Sable turned around and he saw he was the only African man in line. "But I can be of real service to your company, if you would let me show you . . ." he continued.

"You deaf, boy? I said we ain't hiring you. You 'bout as bad as that Indian, Choctaw. Now get!"

Gathering up his pride, Du Sable walked out of the office. Once outside, he got to thinking. Maybe this was a blessing in disguise. If *they* were going up to St. Louis to trap and trade, why couldn't he? All he needed was someone who knew the country. But who? Then a sudden illumination came to him—that Indian named Choctaw!

For several days Du Sable hung around the docks, asking the whereabouts of Choctaw. One evening Du Sable went to a local tavern for dinner. Just as he was about to enter, he was knocked down by a man's body that came flying out the front door.

"You don't talk to Choctaw like that, *ever!*" said the big, strapping Indian filling up the doorway.

The man hurried away, stumbling and running. Du Sable got up, dusted himself off, and approached the angry Indian.

"You're Choctaw?"

"Who are you?" asked Choctaw suspiciously.

"My name is Du Sable. I need a guide."

Choctaw searched Du Sable's face like he had lost something in it. The Indians do this to determine if a man is honest. When he was satisfied that Du Sable was an honest man, he smiled. "Where do you want to go?"

"St. Louis," said Du Sable.

"Hah!" Choctaw said. "If you want to go to St. Louis, we've got a lot of work to do."

Early the next morning, the two men began to chop down large cottonwood trees, from which they constructed a boat. Choctaw rounded up some guns, ammunition, and supplies, and soon they were ready to go.

Jacques, whose leg had partly healed by now, saw them off at the wharf. "Take care of yourself, my friend." he said.

"I'm sorry you can't go," Du Sable said. Jacques had decided to return to France to rest until his leg was completely healed.

"I'm sorry, too," Jacques said. "I'll pray for your success, and maybe someday soon we'll toast each other in Paris."

As Jacques watched, the two men disappeared upriver, their backs bent as they strained to pole their boat against the current.

They pushed onward for weeks, watching the land around them change like the colors of a rainbow. They came to St. Louis and spent several days there. Then they headed off again up the great river. About a week later, Choctaw motioned to Du Sable to pole the boat to shore.

"We need to make camp up ahead," said Choctaw. The men rowed their boat to shore and built a fire.

"Are we getting close?" Du Sable asked.

"Soon the river will get wider. Then we will see white water. We will be close then," said Choctaw.

The campfire warmed Du Sable's sore hands as he watched a beautiful sunset that reminded him of his homeland.

"We are in the land of the great chief Pontiac," said Choctaw.

"Who is this Pontiac you speak so highly of?" asked Du Sable.

"He is a great chief, like your king. He fights the British, who are trying to take his land and harm his people. He is a peaceful man, but white men will not listen to talk of peace—only of war, gold, and fur," said Choctaw.

Du Sable studied the Indian very carefully and noticed a different sound in his voice when he spoke of the British. "Will there be a war with the British?" he asked.

"Before I came to New Orleans, my people, the Choctaws, got word that Pontiac wanted to know who would stand by him if he fought the British. Many Indian nations like the Miamis, Illinois, Chippewas, Potawatomies, Hurons, Shawnees, and the Choctaws said they would stand with Pontiac," he said proudly.

At that moment both men got quiet. Something was rustling in the bushes. As he reached for his gun, Du Sable's arm was gripped by a strong hand, and he felt cold steel pressed against his throat. Choctaw, too, struggled as three Indians held him down. They were taken with their hands tied behind them and placed in a canoe. Choctaw spoke in the Indian's tongue, but their captors said nothing and just kept rowing.

Du Sable turned around and saw two more canoes behind them also filled with Indians. Thoughts of escape raced through his mind, but he was wedged between two big Indians who kept a close eye on him. Pulling into shore, the Indians led both men to a village, where they were placed in a tent and tied back to back.

Two days went by. On the third, five Indians walked into the tent, untied Choctaw's and Du Sable's feet, picked them up by the arms, and led them outside. Without saying a word, the Indians marched them to the far end of the village, to a cabin that was bigger than anything Du Sable had ever seen. Du Sable looked at Choctaw for answers, but Choctaw only returned the glance with a shrug of his shoulders. Then a tall brave came out and motioned them in. Inside, the cabin was lined with a rich tapesty of furs hanging from the walls.

At the end of the cabin, fifteen of the tallest and meanest-looking Indians stood in front of a platform with their arms crossed and eyes locked straight ahead. Du Sable and Choctaw were led up front. Finally, the Indians standing in front of the platform sat down. One tall, graceful Indian mounted the platform with the ease of a deer running through a forest. Du Sable knew he was in the presence of someone important, so he was not surprised to see Choctaw bow his head and turn to him whispering, "Pontiac." Du Sable instantly lowered his head.

Word had spread like a prairie fire that the British were out to assassinate Pontiac. The Illinois Indians had taken special care to see that no harm came to their chief. They had caught two other strangers in the weeks before Choctaw and Du Sable were captured. When those two had admitted they worked for the British, Pontiac had had them killed. Naturally, he was suspicious of Choctaw and Du Sable, too. Choctaw was having problems speaking their tongue, and Du Sable saw that things were not going well by the way all of them kept mumbling and pointing. Du Sable figured that if Pontiac was against the British, it was possible that he might be on the side of the French, which meant there was a slight possibility that he spoke the language.

"O great Pontiac," Du Sable blurted out, "I am a Frenchman. We come in peace and ask your protection!" The room went so quiet you could hear a cat purr. Pontiac waved his hand, and the others moved aside. Du Sable could see from the chief's face that he was familiar with some of the words. Pontiac signaled for a young Indian boy standing by the wall to come over. Then Pontiac whispered into his ear and the young boy spoke to Du Sable in French. A smile as wide as the state of Texas swept across Du Sable's face. The Indian boy had told him that his father wanted him to come closer. See, Indians had a way of looking a man in the eye, and Pontiac could tell right away if that man was a liar or a man of truth. When Du Sable stepped closer, Pontiac stared in his eyes, then smiled.

"He does not have the eyes of a liar," Pontiac said to the young boy, who repeated those words to Du Sable and the others. After three lightning-fast claps of Pontiac's hands, Du Sable and Choctaw were untied. The chief wanted to know more about this African man whose skin was as dark as his own.

"How are you called?" he asked.

"I am Jean Baptiste Pointe Du Sable."

"Listen, then, Mr. Jean Baptiste Pointe Du Sable. My people want only peace, but the white faces bring war and killing. This is a great land. It belongs to none of us. It is the land of the Great Spirit. We must protect it, not destroy it for gold and furs."

"I agree with what you say," Du Sable responded. "I, too, have been at the mercy of white adventurers. When I was young my mother was killed by Spanish pirates. We must all try to share together and live in peace."

Pontiac smiled when he heard Du Sable say this. The chief had heard many white men speak, and had heard as many lies as there are armadilloes in Texas. He knew that this young black Frenchman spoke with a true tongue.

This meeting marked the beginning of a friendship between the young Du Sable and the fifty-year-old chief. During the next two years, Du Sable was seldom away from Pontiac's side. The younger man was entranced by the old chief. There was something magical about him, and he could keep you spellbound with his stories. From him, Du Sable learned much about the background of the Illinois Indian.

Du Sable also sharpened his hunting skills, learned how to

trap, and ride wild horses. When it was time to continue on up the Mississippi, Du Sable had become a woodsman ready to make a fortune in the fur business. The Indians had taught him well, from how to track animals as big as buffaloes to those as small as an otter.

"I know you must go," said Pontiac to Du Sable, who now understood the language much better. "You are like a son to me. Be careful of the British, for they have run the French away and now are the enemy to you and my people."

"I will keep watch, great warrior, and I hope to see you again," said Du Sable.

This was the last time Du Sable ever saw Pontiac alive. A few short weeks after Du Sable moved on downriver to St. Louis, Pontiac was captured by the British and killed.

For Du Sable time now whistled past like a flock of wild geese heading south. He had done well for himself; he was a respected hunter and trapper, and he was well known by all the Indians around the Lake Michigan area. Choctaw had gone back to his own people some time ago, and Du Sable had built his business on his own. He reflected on occasion about his boyhood friend Jacques and their trip to New France. Because he was more settled now, Du Sable decided it was time to find a wife and a piece of land to call his own. He had made friends with a young captain in Peoria, Illinois, named Maillet, who owned some land around the Old Fort Peoria in that area. He had heard the place was for sale and decided to drop in for a look.

When he rode into Peoria he went directly to Captain Maillet's home.

"Jean Baptiste—come in!" said Maillet. "I haven't seen you in some time. How have you been?"

"I'm fine. I'm up here to find out if that piece of land near Old Fort Peoria is still for sale" said Du Sable.

REFLECTIONS OF A BLACK COWBOY

"Oh, so the restless Du Sable wants to buy land now? Let's see, you must have your eye on a bride, am I right?" laughed Maillet.

"Perhaps. Well, is it for sale?" continued Du Sable. "Of course, my friend, it is for sale, and I'll sell it to you for almost nothing," Maillet said with a big smile.

In the spring of 1772, Du Sable, with deed in hand, walked among flowers and long grasses that covered his property along the banks of Lake Michigan. While he was proudly surveying his land he discovered an old broken-down log cabin that was in pretty bad shape. When he walked inside, a rusty tin plate and cup were on a chewed-up wooden table. The floor was rotten, and one of his feet went through it while he tiptoed around. Still, he liked the place and thought, "With a little bit of work this place could be all right."

When Du Sable set up camp on his new property, he noticed that many a traveler passed by, going either to Canada or coming from there on their way to the Mississippi Valley. It didn't take him long to figure out that a trading post on his property would do very good business. He rebuilt the old log cabin, turning it into a trading post, and his business took off like a skyrocket on the Fourth of July. He was doing so well that he built a large family house, a bake house, a dairy, a smokehouse, a stable, a workshop, and a horse-powered mill. This all took some time, but when he was finished he stood back with his chest poked out in pride. Now he felt ready for a wife. In 1774 he married a Potawatomi woman named Kittihawa and convinced the entire Potawatomi village to move onto his land. The trading post, his home, and the farm became the first buildings ever in this new place called Eschikagou.

Du Sable led a prosperous life in the fur-trading business as

Chicago's first settler. Then, by 1800, he became restless again, and life in one place no longer appealed to him, so he sold all his property to a man named Jean Lalime. Some people think Du Sable moved because of disappointment about being voted down by the Miami, Shawnee, Chippewa, Delaware, and Potawatomi as their council chief. He'd known these Indians for many years, so when they voted against him he took it pretty hard. After moving on, his life took more turns than a Kansas tornado. Finally, in 1809, his wife died and Du Sable moved farther south, to St. Charles, Missouri. The next nine years took their toll on this once-proud man. He had seen much of the world, Old and New, tasted adventure, and had made a name for himself as a gentleman among the Indians and a businessman among the traders. I guess you could say he had lived his life as full as a basket of apples during harvest time. On August 28, 1818, Jean Baptiste Pointe Du Sable passed away and was buried in the St. Boromeo cemetery in St. Charles. He left behind a daughter named Suzanne and a granddaughter named Eula-lie. By then, the little town he founded, Eschikagou, or Chicago, had begun to grow. It hasn't stopped growing to this day.

The Old Cowboy went on staring into the dying flames of the fireplace. Sundown yawned and growled a little, then rested his head, with one ear perked, back on his paws. "You know, Sundown," the Old Cowboy said, as he got up to put another log on the fire, "looking at Chicago today, full of people moving fast, its hundreds of shops filled with clothes from all over the world, and businesses booming with every gadget you can think of, you'd never know it was all started by a young black man with a sense of adventure and a love of the sea."

JIM BECKWOURTH: MOUNTAIN MAN AND INDIAN CHIEF

T*he Old Cowboy jumped out of his chair like a ghost had chased him in a bad dream. Dazed, he looked around his cabin for a minute as though he didn't know where he was. When he saw Sundown gnawing on a prized smoked buffalo rib, he suddenly came down to earth.*

"Why . . . where did you get that from, boy?" he asked. Then he remembered that there was only one place the old yellow mutt could have swiped a juicy morsel like that—the smokehouse. The Old Cowboy rushed out to check the smokehouse and found it just as he had left it, minus one buffalo rib.

"Well, I reckon you deserve it, Sundown," he said, returning to the cabin. "Having to put up with me and all." As the Old Cowboy began preparing the rest of the Christmas feast for Two

Hawks and his brothers, Sundown kept gnawing on the buffalo rib like it was his first meal in weeks. All of a sudden the way Sundown grabbed onto that rib reminded the Old Cowboy of someone and he said, "Sundown, there was one fella whose buffalo ribs you probably would have liked even better than mine—Jim Beckwourth, a proud black man, once chief of the Crow Indians, and one of the bravest mountain men ever to set foot in the Rocky Mountains.

They say Jim was born April 26, 1798, on a plantation in Fredericksburg, Virginia. His father was a white man who was a major in the Revolutionary War. Not much is known about Jim's mother, other than she was a slave to his father. Jim was the second oldest of thirteen children, and he had a lot of spunk as a child.

In 1806, when Jim was just eight, the family up and moved, slaves and all, to St. Louis, Missouri. Jim's father searched around and decided on a stretch of land outside of St. Louis between the fork of the Mississippi and the Missouri rivers, just twelve miles below St. Charles, Missouri. He called this place Beckwourth Settlement. At that time that part of Missouri was nothing but wilderness, full of Indians and wild game. Jim noticed that the people he met in St. Louis spoke different kinds of languages, French and Spanish tongues he eventually had to learn.

These were exciting times for a young boy. Not only had he traveled to another part of the country, but he was learning a lot from watching how the French and Spanish got along with the Indians. See, the French and Spanish didn't like those newcomers, called Americans, who were interfering with their trade setup with the Indians. They would barter ammunition, beads, blankets, guns, and "firewater" (alcohol) for some of the most beautiful animal pelts in the whole country. Then they shipped the pelts down the Mississippi to New Orleans and sold them for a bundle of dough to merchants who sold them to wealthy folks back in France or Spain. So you can see why the French and Spanish grew edgy as these new Americans moved into their territory.

Jim, his family, and the other men and women in their group were fast learners when it came to surviving in this new land. For safety's sake, people living in Beckwourth Settlement had to count on one another for protection from hostile Indians. See, the Indians didn't mind sharing the land with the French or the Spanish, but the British and the Americans gave the Indians a hard time. The British decided that the land belonged to them, and believed that the Indians were living on it without British permission. The Americans were a lot like the British. They grabbed more and more land and pushed the Indians farther and farther into a corner until the Osages, Chippewas, Potawatomies, and others in the area had had enough. War often broke out between the Indians, the British, and the American settlers. This friction just got worse after President Jefferson bought a large piece land, known as the Jefferson Purchase or sometimes as the Louisiana Purchase, east of the Mississippi.

Jim grew up faster than weeds in an unkempt garden. He was allowed to roam the countryside around Beckwourth Settlement on his horse, Buster, but one day when he was out for a ride over to a neighbor's house he met with a rude shock. He found the door at the neighbor's place swinging open. Inside he saw his playmate Sonny and Sonny's father, mother, and eight brothers and sisters all dead. They had been killed and scalped by Indians. Jim hurried back to Beckwourth Settlement and was able to warn his family about the Indian threat just before they were attacked by the same group. Because of Jim's courage, his family managed to shoot their way out of this Indian trap.

The slaughter of his friend's family had an effect on Jim. He acted more grown up than his older brothers, and he developed a temper. One day, his father looked at him and decided that Jim now needed some schooling, so he sent him off to a school in St. Louis.

Jim attended school for four years in St. Louis and then, around 1812, when he was fourteen, he left school to work as an apprentice blacksmith under a white man named George Casner.

"You'll work till I say ya stop, and you'll do as you're told; you understand, boy?" demanded the stern Mr. Casner.

"I understand," said Jim, without ever taking his eyes off Mr. Casner's face. Jim didn't like the way this man spoke to him, but he figured he was there to learn a trade, so he decided to put up with it. After five years, he had had enough.

By nineteen Jim had become something of a ladies' man. Tall, lean, and strong looking, with thick black hair that hung down past his ears and a dark copper-brown complexion, Jim was something to behold.

It wasn't long before a young damsel named Francine roped him in.

"Where you been?" Mr. Casner shouted as Jim returned to the blacksmith shop at the crack of dawn. "This is the third night you ain't been in!"

"I was busy," said Jim as he brushed past his boss.

"You know the rules. You're still under my supervision, and you'll mind my rules. You stay in every night after you finish your work—you hear me?" he yelled to Jim upstairs in his room.

Mr. Casner had been working Jim pretty hard for the last year, and his business was showing profits, money that Jim never shared. Well, Jim didn't pay his boss no mind, and he kept on seeing Francine. One morning, after a long evening of dancing with Francine, Jim sashayed into the blacksmith shop like he owned it, which made Mr. Casner madder than a rattlesnake trapped in a box. Jim had no sooner wrapped on his apron than Mr. Casner started giving him a tonguelashing.

"You think you can do as you please, don't you, boy? You need to start minding the rules here," he shouted, moving in close to Jim.

"What I do on my own time is my own business. You ain't my daddy," said Jim, standing his ground.

"I'm gonna do something your daddy should have done a long time ago, boy. I'm gonna whip you like the half-breed you are," said an angry Mr. Casner as he picked up a stick about three feet long.

Jim stood over his boss by a good five inches. Mr. Casner wasn't tall, but he was built like a bulldog, and had broad shoulders and thick arms. Most young boys would have been scared to death. In fact, Mr. Casner was counting on Jim's being a little frightened, but Jim just gave him one of those cold stares like a mountain lion has right before he strikes.

I think Mr. Casner was counting on bluffing Jim to make him behave, but it wasn't working. In order to show Jim who was boss, Mr. Casner made a serious mistake. He raised the stick and swung, aiming to hit Jim around the shoulders. But in the middle of his swing Jim hit him with his left hand and knocked Mr. Casner to the ground.

In all his natural life Mr. Casner had never been hit like that, especially by some young black boy. If people found out that he'd gotten knocked on his backside by Jim he'd never live it down. Jumping right up and still holding the stick, he threw it at Jim, just missing his head. I think Jim had surprised himself with that punch, so he took off back to the roominghouse where he was staying.

Jim didn't wait around to find out what Mr. Casner was going to do. He packed up his stuff and hightailed it out of town. He kicked around the coal mines near the Fever River for a while, but by and by he got a little homesick. Finally, a couple of months later, he returned to Beckwourth Settlement to look in on his family.

When Jim rode into Beckwourth Settlement Jim's father was there waiting for him.

"I heard about you and Mr. Casner," his father said.

"I learned all I could from him" Jim said, "and the last thing I learned was to stand up for myself."

"Won't you go back and finish your apprenticeship?" his father asked.

"I ain't never going back there, Pa," Jim replied.

"What are you going to do, then?" Jim's father asked. "How you going to make a living?"

"I don't know. I hear men talk about a place called New Orleans. Maybe I'll go there. All I know is, I've got to find my own way, and it ain't here."

His father thought long and hard about what his son was saying. He had been nineteen once too. He knew life and adventure was like a tempting juicy, red apple and every young man wanted to take a bite. "You serious about this travel thing, son?" he asked Jim.

"Yes, sir, I am," said Jim.

"It's your call then, son. I wish you well."

Two months later, with seven hundred dollars in his pocket, that his father had given him, Jim leaned over the railing of a flat-bottomed Missouri River keelboat and dreamed of New Orleans as St. Charles, Missouri, came into view. St. Charles was only the first stop on the journey, where the keelboat let him off. He had some time to kill before the next boat shipped out, so he went over to a local tavern and mingled with some folks.

In one of these saloons Jim noticed a black man in the corner telling stories about the Rocky Mountains that held everybody's attention. He moved closer to the crowd to listen to this man weave yarns about trapping wild animals, hunting buffalo, and tracking through virgin territory. The more Jim heard, the more he wanted to know. When this black man finished his stories and got up to leave, he accidentally bumped into Jim.

"Pardon me, sir," said the stranger.

Jim noticed a different sound in his voice, reminding him of the French-speaking people back at the settlement. His curiosity led him to follow the man outside.

"Excuse me, mister," said Jim. "Those stories you told back there—are they really true?"

The handsome older black man looked at young Jim and smiled. "Everything I said about the Rocky Mountains is true. Everything."

"I'd sure like to see it someday," said Jim.

"You may have your chance. A friend of mine named General William Henry Ashley owns the Rocky Mountain Fur Company in St. Louis. I hear he's putting together a party of men to go back to the Rockies and do some hunting. I'm sure he could use a good man. What can you do?" he asked.

"I'm a blacksmith, a good shot, and can handle myself in any situation," bragged Jim.

"Tell him I sent you, and I'm sure he'll give you a job," he said, turning to get on his horse.

"You must forgive my manners, sir. I didn't introduce myself. I'm Jim Beckwourth," said Jim, stretching out his hand.

"I'm Jean Baptiste Pointe Du Sable. My pleasure meeting you," the older man said, shaking Jim's hand, then riding off.

Jim heard the steamboat blow its whistle three times, looked at his seven hundred dollars, and made up his mind right there. "Well, New Orleans, you gonna have to wait. St. Louis, here I come," he said. Then he went over to the livery stable, bought himself a horse, and lit out cross-country to St. Louis.

When he got to St. Louis, it didn't take him long to find the Rocky Mountain Fur Company. The general had a reputation for paying good wages, and men were lined up down the street trying to get jobs. Jim looked at the competition and realized that some of those men had a lot more experience than he did, so he figured to get hired he would have to get ahead of some of the competition. Falling out of line, Jim slipped around back of the Fur Company's building. A door leading inside was slightly open, and he could hear men talking.

"General, we have most of the men we need. We're gonna stop hiring right now," said one of the men.

"This trip is very important, and we'll be gone for some time. You got anybody who can shoe and take care of our horses?" asked the general.

"If you mean did I hire a blacksmith, well, no, I didn't think . . ."

"You didn't think? Did you think *I* was gonna shoe all those pack horses? Find me a blacksmith, now! Is that clear?" shouted the general.

Not being on the shy side, Jim saw his chance and leaped

on it like a coyote on a prairie dog. "You got one now!" he hollered, busting through the back door.

"Who the devil are you?" asked the general.

"My name is Beckwourth, sir. I'm a trained blacksmith and know everything there is to know about shoeing horses," replied Jim.

The general looked Jim over. He was young, thought the general, but Jim had a lot of nerve, and nerve was something the general admired in a man. "How do I know you can do what you say?" asked the general.

"Give me a horse, and I'll show you," said Jim.

Jim shoed four horses faster than a locomotive going downhill with her throttles wide open. "You do good work, Beckwourth. What's your first name?" asked the general.

"Jim, sir." To make sure he nailed this job down, Jim played his trump card. "By the way, a good friend of ours told me to tell you hello," he said to the general.

"Who's that?" the general replied.

"Jean Baptiste Pointe Du Sable," said Jim, with a grin.

The general's eyes lit up like a Texas night sky. "Any friend of Du Sable's is a friend of mine. He's the best darn trapper and hunter I ever saw. When can you start?"

"When do you move out?" asked Jim.

"First thing in the morning we head for the Rocky Mountains," replied the general.

"I'll be ready," said Jim.

Those were some exciting times for a restless young man like Jim Beckwourth. He proved to be very valuable to the hunting party and came to earn the respect of General Ashley. Jim's duties included hunting, trapping, rounding up horses, and, many times, fighting off Indians. He and the general got along pretty well, and Jim saved his life on more than one occasion. What Jim didn't know about trapping he learned from the older men, and he got so good at it you'd have thought he was a born woodsman.

As the hunting party moved farther into the mountains, their survival and success with trapping depended on trading goods with the Indians. If the Sioux, Cheyenne, Flatheads, and Blackfeet didn't like what you had in trade, you didn't get to trap on their hunting ground. Jim learned how to trade with them all and speak their language. But he would fight them, too, if he had to. One problem was that the Indians were looking for fresh horses, and this led to many battles over who could keep horses that were found on the range. This is where Jim proved he was the best of the best when it came to fighting. He'd take on what seemed like ten to fifteen Indians at once. Arrows flew past him and all around him, but none ever touched him. Indians fell to the right and left with every mighty swing of Jim's rifle butt.

This trapping season had reaped a mighty big harvest for the general and the Rocky Mountain Fur Company. On their way back to St. Louis, the pack horses were loaded down with furs of every kind. The men were already counting their money, but before they could spend it they had to get back to St. Louis. The trip back was taking a toll on the food supply. One pint of beans a day was all there was to feed four men. I guess you could say every man's nerves were as raw as fresh meat, and it wouldn't take much to set him off. Jim's job was to shoe the horses, but since he gave personal attention to the general, he only took care of the general's horses. It was cold one morning when the general called Jim over to put new shoes on his horse. "Jim, this old nag needs some new feet," said the general as he dismounted.

"I'll take care of it," said Jim. He got out his hammer and

nails and four new horse shoes and proceeded to shoe the general's horse. He was down to the last nail to place in the fourth shoe when the horse jerked his hoof out of Jim's hand. The horse had been rambunctious all along, and I guess he'd just had enough. Jim grabbed his hoof again, but the horse jerked it out of Jim's hand a second time. Then Jim used an old blacksmith's trick to settle a jittery horse. He took his hand and rubbed the horse's belly a couple of times. For some reason the general was very impatient that day and raised his voice at Jim. "Hurry up; do you know what you're doing?" shouted the general.

Jim dropped the horse's hoof without putting the last nail in the shoe, stood up with rage in his eyes, and threw the hammer on the ground. "There's one more nail left, and if you want it nailed you do it yourself," said Jim.

"Why you rascal. Don't ever talk to me like that. I'll blow your brains out!" said the general as he reached for his rifle. But Jim had already drawn his pistol and had it cocked right at the general's head.

"General, no man treats me that way. Unless you take back those words, you will surely die."

No man had ever drawn a gun on the general before, and he was surprised to see a black man pointing a gun at him, telling him he would die unless he apologized. "I'm sorry, Jim. You're right. I shouldn't have used that kind of language. I was angry and spoke too hastily. But I'll make you pay for daring to draw a gun on me."

"No you won't. I quit, and am never working for you again. Give me my money, and you can take your horse," said Jim.

The general paid Jim what he owed him, and Jim holstered his gun. "Where will you go?" asked the general.

"That's my business," replied Jim as he took his belongings and headed west toward California. The general knew he was losing a good man. Jim had saved his life on many occasions. If he could have taken back those words he would have, but it was too late, and all he could do was watch Jim ride off. It was many years before the two men saw each other again, and when they did Jim had very few words for the general.

Jim Beckwourth was a man who was moved by danger and challenge. When he left the general, Jim took on a series of odd jobs. He hired out as a scout for the U.S. Army, worked as a guide, and did anything he had to to make some money and keep his independence. All was going well for him until 1825, when he met a trapper named William Sublette. By now Jim was in Yellowstone country, which includes parts of Montana and Wyoming. Jim had met Sublette once before, when he had worked with the general, so when he bumped into Sublette at a trading post in the Yellowstone country the two men remembered each other.

"Jim, Jim Beckwourth—how you been?" asked an excited Sublette.

"Just fine. Fancy seeing you in these parts," said Jim.

"You know me—wherever the game goes, that's where I'll be," replied Sublette. "Jim, you got a minute? I've got an idea I want to run by you . . . . There's a lot of money to be made if a man could open up a trading post in Blackfeet territory. I heard they want to do business. I mentioned it to Jim Bridger, but he turned me down. The general told me about your courage and how you handle yourself with the Indians. It's a great opportunity, Jim. What do you say? You in?"

Jim thought about it a while. He knew that if Jim Bridger, a famous white hunter and trapper, had turned it down it had to be dangerous. Jim also knew why Sublette

was having a hard time finding somebody to go with him. The Blackfeet were the most feared Indians in Yellowstone country. You couldn't play around with their hunting grounds. Even if they wanted you there, you always had to watch yourself. Still, Jim couldn't turn down a challenge. "When do we meet the chief?" he grinned.

When they rode into Blackfoot country they were met by a band of braves who took them to their chief. By now Jim had had plenty of experience in dealing with Indians. The Blackfeet could tell that this was a different kind of man, because Jim showed no fear of them. He told the Indians what they wanted to do, and promised that he and his partner would trade fair with them. The Blackfeet agreed, and that season Jim and Sublette acquired twenty-nine packs of the best beaver, in just three weeks. Jim stayed on with Sublette until that itch for something new started up again.

In 1828, Jim and a white trapper friend named Caleb Greenwood were out trapping once when they ran into some Crow Indians. One of the braves kept looking at Jim rather curiously.

"They're trying to figure you out," laughed Greenwood. "Let's have a little fun." Then Greenwood said to the Crow Indian in his native tongue, "You know he is Crow." The Indian stopped and took a close look at Jim. "The Snake Indians call him White Handled Knife. Many years ago the Cheyenne fought the Crows. They killed many braves. They took many women and children," said Greenwood. The Crows looked at each other and remembered this battle. "White Handled Knife was one of the children taken by the Cheyennes. He is the son of a strong warrior brave," said Greenwood. What had started out as a joke turned out to be taken as a serious story by the Crows.

Weeks later, Jim was following his traps near the Powder

River, in Crow territory. He wasn't paying much attention when some Crow Indians spotted him and quickly rode back to their village to spread the word that the kidnapped son of the Crow chief had come home. Jim still didn't pay the Indians any mind when fifteen of them rode up to him.

"Come with us, lost son of the brave Crow warrior," one of them said.

At first Jim didn't get it. He knew he wasn't a Crow, but then he remembered the story Greenwood had told about him and decided to play along. He figured that once they got back to the village they would soon find out that he wasn't related to any of them, and they'd all have a big laugh.

As they rode into the Crow village, Jim couldn't believe his eyes. Women and children were all lined up in two rows dressed in their finest clothes. As he got farther into the village, young girls ran up to his horse, reaching out and trying to touch him, while the braves who rode along each side of him pushed them away. The joke had now turned into something more serious. The Crow braves then led Jim to the last teepee, where they stopped.

"This is the wife of Big Bowl. She was there when the Cheyennes took her son. She says that if you are her true son, she will know," said one of the Crow braves.

Jim knew his goose was cooked now, and he was getting pretty nervous. Drums began beating in the background as the wife of Big Bowl came out of the tent. She was a lovely elderly lady with snow-white hair that hung down her back. Jim had lived in the Yellowstone country for some time and knew the language, so when one of the braves told him to get off his horse he obeyed. Standing there in front of all those Crow Indians, Jim figured that his chances for escape were getting slimmer by the minute.

"If you are truly my son, you will have a mole on one of

your eyelids,'' said the woman. She pulled Jim's head down and had him close his eyes as she searched for the secret mole. Then the wife of Big Bowl examined Jim's eyelids like a hungry eagle searching for his prey. ''Yes, you are my son, my son, you have returned!'' she shouted. She had in fact found a tiny mole on Jim's left eyelid. Then her daughters and other sons accepted Jim and greeted him as if he was their lost brother. If they had doubts about him they didn't show it, for Jim soon proved he was worthy of being called a Crow.

The Indians dressed him in leggins, moccasins, and other clothes befitting a true Crow. Jim was also given other rights, including his pick of the young Indian maidens in the village as his bride. He chose Still Water, the chief's oldest daughter.

No sooner had Jim become a Crow, than he was thrown into the middle of fighting all their enemies. For Jim Beckwourth, fighting was as natural as riding a horse was to an Indian. He lived with the Crows for over six years and fought their fiercest enemy, the Blackfeet. It was always Jim who led the Crows into battle and inflicted the most pain on their enemies. Soon his bravery became legendary in Yellowstone country, and he was eventually made chief of the Crow nation. Six years was a long time for Jim Beckwourth to stay in one place, and sure enough, soon that restless fever began stirring in his blood. One night he just packed his belongings and took off to California. Later he moved to New Mexico and opened up a small trading post for a while. After making enough money to move on, he left that business too. In 1844 Jim rode into Monterey, California, and hired out to a man named Captain Denny to carry dispatches during the Mexican War. He worked odd jobs here and there, but it was for his leading a wagon train of settlers across the Rockies to California that his name will forever be remembered. In April 1850, after crossing the Rockies, Jim noticed what looked like a valley that cut southward from Reno, Nevada, through the Sierra Nevadas. This discovery became named the Beckwourth Pass. It saved travelers many days when crossing the Rocky Mountains to California.

The years following Jim's discovery of the Beckwourth Pass brought more restlessness and his life took more turns than the Snake River. In 1852 he tried ranching in Westport, Missouri, and in 1862 he tried to serve his country by volunteering to fight in the Civil War, even though he was sixty-four years old. In 1866 a Colonel Henry B. Carrington sent word to Jim that his services were needed.

"I hear you been looking for me," said Jim as he walked into the colonel's office.

"Yes, I have. I understand you know these parts like the back of your hand," said the colonel.

"Better than that," said Jim.

The colonel was sizing up Jim as he spoke to him. He knew this strong black man was no spring chicken, but there was still a fierceness about him that the colonel liked and respected.

"We're having some problem with the Crows in Montana. I think they'll be going on the warpath soon. I heard that once you were their chief. If you can talk them out of this war, you'll save many lives. You want the job?" asked the colonel.

"Give me one trooper, and I'll be back with a peace treaty," said Jim.

When the Crows saw Jim again, they were torn between joy from not having seen him in years and anger, because he had run off suddenly. No sooner had he ridden into the village than chief Big Bowl came out of his teepee to greet him.

"You have come back, my son," said the chief.

Jim gave him the Crow greeting and said, "I have come to seek council with the elders to talk of peace between the Crows and the white soldiers."

The chief eyed the trooper standing alongside Jim. He wasn't pleased that Jim was siding against his own to talk peace with the white man. "You may come in. He must stay out. I will call the elders, and we will go to the lodge to talk," said the chief. For three days and nights Jim and the Crow council met. On the fourth day, something happened. One of the Crow chiefs walked outside the lodge and spoke to a brave. Soon, the drums started beating.

"What's going on?" asked the surprised trooper.

"Our great warrior son is dead," the brave said.

The trooper tried to force his way into the lodge to see what had happened to Jim, but ten Crows blocked the doorway.

"Go tell your leader our son now sleeps with his fathers," said Chief Big Bowl.

The Crows wouldn't tell the trooper anything else about Jim, but he knew that if a fight had broken out he would have heard something, and he hadn't heard a thing. Jumping on his horse, the trooper rode back to Colonel Carrington and reported Jim's strange death.

Nobody knows for sure what happened in that lodge. Some say the Crows killed Jim for siding with their enemy, the white man. Whatever happened, Jim Beckwourth died as had lived—close to danger, like a moth drawn to a flame. He traveled all through this land and left his mark on every man he met.

"Well, Sundown," the Old Cowboy said, "I'd better hurry up and finish making this dinner. Two Hawks and his family will be here in a minute."

Then the Old Cowboy finished making the dinner, and when Two Hawks and his family came over on Christmas day they all had a wonderful feast, and shared gifts after dinner. The Indians have a tradition of bringing gifts when they share special time with friends, and Two Hawks and the Old Cowboy had shared many together. That night they sang traditional songs and told each other stories—and when it came to stories, no one told them better than the Old Cowboy.

GEORGE MCJUNKIN: SCHOLAR AND COWBOY

The morning after Christmas, the Old Cowboy had gotten up early to make coffee for his guests and see them off. Before he had left, Two Hawks had given the Old Cowboy a very special present: an ancient Sioux peace pipe that had once belonged to Two Hawks's great-great-grandfather. This present set the Old Cowboy to thinking about how long the Indian had been here in North America.

"You know, Sundown," he said, "there once was a black man who discovered a whole heap of facts about the history of Indians on this continent just by digging around for bones out in the desert. His name was George McJunkin, and he turned out to be one of those rare people who helped humankind gain a little more understanding of itself.

The way I heard it, Sundown, George was born a slave in Texas, around 1851. He was the property of a white man named John McJunkin. Back in those days a slave took the last name from his white master. George was not your typical young boy growing up on a ranch. He was a slave, but that never stopped him from thinking, and freedom was all he ever thought about.

When George wasn't helping his daddy shoe horses for Master McJunkin, he'd be watching some of the other cowboys break some of the wild mustangs for riding. Young George rode his first wild horse when he was about eleven years old. He and other slave boys would sneak rides on wild horses' backs when the master wasn't looking.

See, slaves weren't allowed to ride horses or go on cattle drives when George was growing up in Texas, because before the Civil War all those jobs belonged to the white cowboys. Then, when the Civil War started, most of the white men left Texas to fight for the South. That didn't leave many white cowboys on the ranches to tame wild horses or shoe them. With white men being as scarce in Texas as a gold tooth in a squirrel's mouth, the door was opened for George's daddy to become head blacksmith on the McJunkin plantation and for young George to ride the wild mustangs.

When the Civil War ended in 1865, and President Lincoln had freed all the slaves, young George was around fourteen and itching to strike out on his own. He understood that he was a free man now, and no longer the property of Master McJunkin. One day, George's daddy eyed his son as the boy stared off into space. He could recognize that faraway look in George's eyes.

''You got somethin' on your mind, George?'' his father asked.

"I'm free, Papa. I know how to ride horses. I even learned from the Mexican cowboys how to swing a rope over a horse's head or snap one under his hind heels at full gallop. There's a need for my kind of work, and now that slaves are free I can go anywhere and find a job. See, papa, I want to be a cowboy."

His father just looked at him for a minute. "Can you read, son? If you want to count for something, you got to know how to read. I know you think there are plenty of jobs right now, with all those longhorned steers roaming loose out here, but mark my word, as soon as those herds thin out, the white men will take all the regular cowboy jobs for themselves. I learned to read from the Bible and you can, too."

"Ain't we supposed to be getting a school soon?" asked George.

"I wouldn't bet my worn-out shoes on that ever happenin'. If you want to learn how to read, you'll pick up that Bible and read it like I did. Keep in mind, don't depend on no white man to do anything for ya that ya can do for yourself!"

George listened to his daddy and decided it wasn't quite time to run off just yet, not until he could read.

George picked up the Bible and began to read. The more he read, the thirstier he got for knowledge, and the more he learned, the more he wondered about the life of a cowboy. For a young black man tasting the meat of freedom, it was getting harder to stay in one place, especially on a ranch where he had once been a slave. Two slow years passed until one afternoon when a bunch of white cowboys rode up to Mr. McJunkin's ranch with some wild mustangs. "Just put 'em over there in the south end of the corral!" shouted McJunkin to one of the cowboys.

"You got yourself some mighty fine steeds, Mr. McJunkin. They goin' to be tough to break," said one of the other cowboys as he rode out of the corral.

When George saw the cowboys ride up, he stopped what he was doing and just watched the way they handled those horses. He had been riding a few wild broncos at a ranch down the road where all the cowboys were Mexicans. George could hold his own pretty good, but he'd never ridden in front of any of the white cowboys or Mr. McJunkin.

Once the cowboys had taken a rest, it was time to start breaking some of those mustangs. This is what young George had been waiting for. He liked to watch some of the better cowboys ride those wild mustangs until they just trotted around the corral like house puppies. Many of the cowboys placed side bets on who could ride the longest without being thrown off, making a contest out of a hard day's work. While the men were breaking the horses, George slowly walked over to the corral and leaned up against the fence to get a better look.

"Ain't you got chores to do, boy?" joshed one of the white cowboys.

George watched a cowboy riding a chestnut-brown stallion get thrown off and almost trampled as he ran and jumped over the corral fence. Before he knew it the words slipped from his mouth. "I bet I can stay on him!"

"You can do what?"

"I can ride that stallion," said George.

When the white cowboy heard that, he figured it was time for all of them to have a good laugh on young George.

"Hey, fellas! This boy thinks he can ride. I say we give him a chance!"

They laughed so loud that Mr. McJunkin came out of the

house to see what all the commotion was about. George didn't expect to be part of a show and be made a fool of, but he had enough confidence in himself to know that wasn't going to happen.

"Bring that stallion over here. If this boy says he can stay on, let's see if he's a boy or a man," said the cowboy.

A lump the size of Texas was forming in the pit of George's stomach when he saw his daddy come walking out of the livery stable, carrying an iron clamp with a smoking horseshoe still in it. He looked over and saw his young son standing in the corral while white men laughed and pointed at him like he was a clown in a circus. Anger swelled up in George's daddy like a mighty river about to overflow its banks, and he walked slowly over to the corral. Once the white men saw him coming, the laughter stopped. George had climbed on top of the fence near the gate, getting ready to leap on the stallion's back.

"George! What are you doing!" shouted his father.

George had mustered up all the courage he could. Looking at his father, he shouted, "Watch me!" and leaped on the stallion's back.

What started out to be a joke turned into a lesson on wild bronco riding given by a young black man to some seasoned white cowboys. Nobody laughed now as that wild stallion tried with all his might to shake young George off his back. He jumped up high in the air, spinning like a top, but George held on. The stallion tried ramming him into the corral fence, but George had learned his lessons well from the Mexican cowboys on how to turn a horse in the opposite direction without fighting it. When the stallion reared up on its hind feet, George heard a loud yell. "Ride 'em, young fella! Ride 'em!" shouted the white cowboys.

George's daddy's anger had turned to pride as he watched

his son stick to that stallion like peanut butter to bread. A smile creeped across his face as he joined in with the others. "Ride him, son! Show him who's boss!"

Young George showed them all who was boss, including Mr. McJunkin. That stallion was starting to get the message that he wasn't gonna throw this rider, but he still had one more trick to play. He stopped bucking and started galloping around the corral. The other cowboys were yelling and whistling for George. That's when George lost his concentration and eased up on the pressure his legs were putting on the sides of the horse. The stallion bucked and turned right, but George went left and landed on his rear end. This time everybody laughed, but they didn't poke fun at George after that. He earned their respect and showed them that being able to stay on the back of a wild stallion had nothing to do with the color of a man's skin.

His daddy was proud of what his son had done that day, but from then on when he looked at George he could tell it would just be a matter of time before he'd be saying good-bye. That day came early one morning when he found George's horse saddled up and ready to ride. "You heading out without saying good-bye?" George's papa asked.

"I figured it would be better if I left quietly," George said. "I'd get word back later about where I was staying."

"Well, I'm glad I caught you," his father said. "Sometimes these little journeys have a way of stretching into years."

"Well, I guess I'll be seeing you," George said. He had never said good-bye to his father before, and the words stuck in his throat.

"I want you to remember something, son. Read the Bible and everything else you can get your hands on. You're free now, and that's something no man can take away from you."

George rode for about a week, and before long he found an outfit that took him in. "Rider coming!" a cowboy shouted as George galloped into camp. A big strapping white man stood up from a bunch of cowboys sitting around eating supper. George dismounted, gathered himself, and bravely walked over to where the others were sitting. "I'm looking for work, sir. Are you hiring?"

The trail boss walked around George checking him out like you'd do a prime stallion for breeding. He liked what he saw in George. "Today must be your lucky day, young fella. We need a wrangler. So if you want the job, it's yours."

"Yes, sir!" shouted George.

"Then check in with Charlie over there and he'll tell you what to do." George was happier than a young colt in a field of hay, even though being a wrangler wasn't quite what he had in mind. However, it was a place to start. In time, he reckoned he would move up to being a real cowboy.

As a wrangler, George had to help the cook prepare food for the cowboys and take care of their horses on the long trail drives. Caring for the horses during cattle drives was a serious responsibility. It kept the cowboys constantly moving by providing them with fresh mounts.

They had been on the trail for two months headed for Dodge City, Kansas, when a rumbling noise like a man stumbling into tables in a dark room filled the night sky. The horses started getting restless, and the cattle began moving anxiously in different directions. Suddenly the flash of distant lightning illuminated the sky, followed seconds later by the low rumble of thunder. The cattle and horses spooked.

"Stampede! Stampede!" shouted two cowboys on guard duty. Everyone else jumped to their feet. It was pitch black and George could barely find his mount. Searching for the stirrups and reins like blind man groping for his cane,

George leaped onto his horse's back. Another flash of lightning showed him that the herd was forming a huge circle. He rode lickety-split to head them off.

"Turn 'em right!" shouted a cowboy over the thundering roar of hoofbeats. Like a bullet, George headed for the lead steer. Snapping his rope like a whip, he turned the lead steer right, and the herd followed. The scattered animals then ran themselves into a full circle. Any danger of losing them now was over. The stampede had ended almost as quickly as it had started, except for one thing: George McJunkin had proved his worth that night. From then on his duties changed from wrangler to punching cattle. He had finally become a real cowboy.

George's adventures as a cowboy led him all over Texas and parts of New Mexico. From his humble beginnings as a wrangler he worked as a cowpuncher on different ranches and finally ended up managing the eight-thousand-acre Crowfoot Ranch. As foreman of that ranch George was always busy. I guess that's why he never looked his age. At fifty years of age, he weighed a hair under 160 pounds, but he was still as strong as an ox. He never found time to go to school, but that didn't stop him from learning everything he could, especially about some odd-shaped rocks on the Crowfoot Ranch.

Right after a heavy flood on the ranch late in the summer of 1908, George took a cowhand out with him to check on property damage. They came to one gully in which mud was piled up over three feet high.

"Look at that fence!" said the cowhand.

George turned and saw that it was dangling in the mud that had broken it, ripping it off the post. As they rode on, George noticed something white sticking out of the black mud. "Hold up!" said George. Dismounting, he walked

over to the bone. Taking his barb-wire cutters, he scraped the dirt from around an old bone that had lain ten feet below the ground.

"What is it?" asked the cowhand.

"I don't rightly know. Maybe a buffalo bone, but if it is, it's the biggest buffalo bone I ever saw," said George.

He dug around and found some smaller bones, then tied the big bone to his saddle and headed on back to the ranch. That night he stayed up searching through his books trying to find answers to the mystery of this huge bone. Whenever he went back to the spot where he had found the bone, he would find more skulls, and ribs of humans and animals that looked different from anything he'd ever read about. The cowboys around Crowfoot didn't care much about old bones, so George just had to wonder to himself about his finding.

Four years later, George attended a county fair in Raton, New Mexico, where he had entered his chuck wagon in an old-time chuck wagon contest. He had driven the contraption forty miles from Crowfoot Ranch to Raton to enter the contest. When he got there, the roads had weakened one of the wagon wheels so much that he had to take it to a blacksmith shop to be fixed. This place was run by a man named Carl Schwachheim.

"What can I do for you, mister?" Schwachheim said, eyeing George's chuck wagon.

"I need my left wheel tightened up," said George.

"Mighty find chuck wagon, sir, if I do say so myself," said Carl.

"Thank you," George said, as he wandered to the front of the shop. There he noticed a pair of the biggest elk antlers he'd ever seen. "Those bull elk antlers are huge. Where did you get them?" he asked.

"Up on Johnson mesa. They're 'bout the biggest I've ever seen."

"Well, they ain't the biggest bones I've seen. I found a bone near Folsom that is big enough to hold those two antlers up," said George.

When Carl heard that, he stopped what he was doing. "Where is this place?"

George began to tell him how and where he had found the huge bone and other smaller ones. He even had a name for this place; he called it the Bone Pit. George discovered that Carl was a collector, too, and the two of them spent the whole time talking about bones. Carl showed George a diary of all his findings—from birds to flowers and anything else he had found in the New Mexico plains.

"When I can find the time, I'd like to come out and see this Bone Pit of yours," said Carl.

"You're welcome any time," said George. That was truly George's lucky day, he got his wagon fixed, made a new friend, won the chuck-wagon contest, and for his prize got a new rifle and the honor of leading the parade.

Time raced by like a chicken running from a hungry fox. Three years had passed since George had spoken to Carl Schwachheim, and so far the two men hadn't connected. The owner of the Crowfoot Ranch had put the place up for sale, and George had partially retired to a home he had built for himself in Folsom. His body was starting to sag like old timbers in an abandoned mine, and he had to rely on a cane when he walked. Riding a horse gave him nothing but pain.

"George, you ought to let the doctor take a look at that leg," a cowhand told him one day.

"I'll be all right," replied a hobbling George. But he wasn't all right; a few months later George had to sell his house in Folsom and move into a hotel. He was too weak to care for himself. On January 1922, George McJunkin died and was buried in the Folsom cemetery.

George died without ever knowing the power his Bone Pit discovery would have in changing how scientists thought about early man in America. He didn't know the powerful role that his chance meeting with Carl Schwachheim would play in bringing his discovery to light. Nearly four months after George died, Carl got some time off and brought a group of men with him to visit the Bone Pit. He followed a map that George had given him.

After digging for a while the group found bones bigger than the elk horns Carl had in front of his blacksmith shop. It wasn't until they were able to get these bones to the Colorado Museum of Natural History four years later that interest in the site began to spread like a wild prairie fire throughout the science community.

On August 2, 1927, Carl found a spear head stuck between two ribs of a bison, a very old and extinct animal similar to a buffalo. This proved that man had been roaming the New Mexico plains at the time that bisons lived there— well over 10,000 years ago. Up until George McJunkin's discovery of the Bone Pit, now called the Folsom Site, scientists had believed that the North American Indian had come to America only 3,000 years ago. What George's discovery proved was that the Indian had been here much longer than that.

This was a heck of a discovery and would have made George McJunkin, the curious cowpuncher from Texas, mighty proud.

"Well, Sundown," the Old Cowboy said as he put the ancient Sioux peace pipe away for safekeeping in a drawer, *"George is a good example of how a man can get a whole heap of enjoyment out*

of life by never giving up faith in himself. You see, nobody could stop George from poking around in things he didn't know much about and trying to figure out how they worked. I think that's what makes you and me tick, too, don't you think?"

Sundown just yawned and flopped down near the Old Cowboy's bed. A winter's night was falling, and as a fat cornbread moon rose over the mountains a lonely wolf's howl pierced the darkness. The Old Cowboy cocked an ear to listen, and smiled. "Sundown," he said, "that lonesome old wolf's howl reminds me of something. Did I ever tell you about the time . . ."

BIBLIOGRAPHY

Beckwourth, Jim. *The Autobiography of Jim Beckwourth.* New York: Harper & Brothers, 1856.

Bontemps, Arna, and Jack Conroy. *Anyplace But Here.* New York: Hill & Wang, 1945.

Dobler, Lavinia, and Edgar Toppina. *Pioneers and Patriots.* Garden City, New York: Doubleday, 1965.

Folsom, Franklin. *The Life and Legend of George McJunkin, Black Cowboy.* Nashville and New York: Thomas Nelson, 1973.

Graham, Shirley. *Jean Baptiste Pointe Desable: Founder of Chicago.* New York: Julian Messner, 1953.

Katz, William. *The Black West.* Seattle: Open Hand, 1987.

Quaife, Milo M. "Chicago and the Old Northwest."
Unpublished Ph.D. dissertation. University of Chicago,
1913.

Stewart, Paul W. *Black Cowboys*. Bloomfield, Co.: Phillips,
1986.

---

*I want to give special thanks to Mr. Franklin Folsom for his book *The
Life and Legend of George McJunkin*. His research and accounts of
George's young life were a tremendous help to me in developing the
character of George McJunkin. In addition, finding suitable informa-
tion on Jean Baptiste Pointe Du Sable would have been extremely
difficult without the creatively written account of his life by Mrs.
Shirley Graham entitled *Jean Baptiste Pointe Desable: Founder of Chicago.*